Exploration Into
JAPAN

RICHARD TAMES

Chelsea House Publishers
Philadelphia

First published in hardback edition in 2001
by Chelsea House Publishers, a subsidiary of
Haights Cross Communications. All rights reserved.
Printed and bound in China.

First published in the UK in 1995 by
Belitha Press Limited, London House,
Great Eastern Wharf, Parkgate Road,
London SW11 4NQ, England

Editor: Kate Scarborough
Designer: Simon Borrough
Picture Researcher: Juliet Duff
Series consultant: Shane Winser, Royal Geographical Society,
London
Consultant: Akiko Motoyoshi

First printing
1 3 5 7 9 8 6 4 2

The Chelsea House World Wide Web address is
http://www.chelseahouse.com

Library of Congress Cataloging-in-Publication Data applied for.

ISBN: 0-7910-6023-3

Picture acknowledgments:
Ancient Art and Architecture Collection: 18 bottom, 28 left,
29 top. Asashi Shimbun Photos, Tokyo: 29 bottom.
Bridgeman Art Library: 14 bottom, Tokugawa Reimeikai
Foundation, Tokyo, 37 bottom Giraudon/Musee d'Orsay,
Paris. British Museum: 12 top. Comstock Photos: 9
bottom left. E.T. Archive: 8 center Freer Gallery of Art, 22,
23 bottom, 30 bottom British Museum, 35 Postal Museum,
Frankfurt, 36 top right Private Collection, 38 top, 39 top,
41 top. Mary Evans Picture Library: 34 top, 36 center, 40
bottom. Werner Forman Archive: title page, 2, 3 National
Museum, Kyoto, 7 left Private Collection, 10, 11 bottom,
13 top, 21 bottom British Museum, 24 bottom Kuroda
Collection Japan, 25 bottom Tempus Collection, London,
27 top Basho Kenshokai, Ueno. Fukuzawa Memorial Center
for Modern Japanese Studies, Keio University: 32 top.
Robert Harding Picture Library: 11 top and 19 center Nigel
Blythe, 17 both, 32 bottom. Michael Holford: 9 top, 19
bottom, 30-31. Hulton Deutsch Collection: 24 top, 33, 34
bottom, 39 bottom. Hutchison Library: 44 bottom, 45
bottom. Japan Archive: 8 bottom, 15 both, 16 top, 21 top,
42. Japan Information and Cultural Center: 4, 44 top, 45
top. Photri Inc: 41 bottom. Popperfoto: 7 right, 36 top
left, 43. Rijksmuseum voor Volkenkunde, Leiden: 29 center.
Richard Tames: 16 bottom, 20, 23 top, 26 both, 27 bottom,
38 bottom.

Previous page: A
pond in one of the
earliest Zen gardens
in Kyoto. The torii
gateway in the
foreground is a
Shinto motif.

This page: The
Shinto god of Hell
holding a scroll.

Contents

A *sculpture of the priest Hoshi, whose face is splitting to reveal a deity.*

1 Exploring Japan

Japan – A Nation Apart?

Japan stands apart, in the physical sense, as a group of islands. The country's borders are set by the sea. Japan's nearest neighbor, Korea, is over 115 miles (190 kilometers) away. The Japanese as a people also stand apart. Most countries in the world have minorities who differ from the majority population by reason of their race, religion, or language. Japan has a population of over 123 million. Adding up all the minorities accounts for only about 2 percent of the population. Christians are the largest religious minority, and the largest ethnic minority are the 700,000 Koreans; but 90 percent of them were born in Japan, and many have never been to Korea or learned to speak Korean. Only since World War II have the Japanese begun to travel overseas in large numbers or had the chance to meet foreigners, especially Westerners, in Japan. For most of their history the Japanese have thought of themselves as a separate – and special – people.

A Language Apart

The Japanese language also helps to make the Japanese feel special, because it is quite different from any other. **Pronunciation** is not difficult for speakers of European languages, but the grammar is extremely complicated. So is the system of writing. Before the Japanese made contact with China, they had no way of writing their language. They took over the Chinese way of writing with characters (*kanji*) but also had to develop two additional syllabaries (*kana*), because Chinese and Japanese are very different languages, both in grammar and in pronunciation. A syllabary is like an alphabet, but the symbols stand for syllables instead of single sounds. To be able to read a Japanese newspaper, you need to know both kana and at least 3,000 characters. In this book Japanese names are given in the Japanese order – surname first.

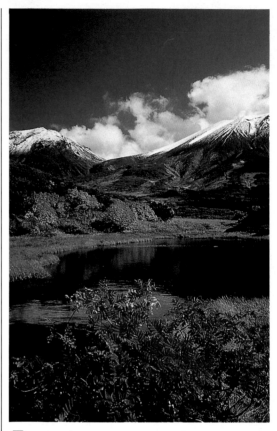

The seasons in Japan are clearly marked, and their changes have always been important subjects for Japanese poets and painters. The climate ranges from subtropical in Okinawa to subarctic in the Kuril Islands.

Japan is an **archipelago** of four main islands and over 4,000 small ones. About four-fifths of the country is mountainous, so most of the population is squeezed onto the coastal plains. Japan's rivers are mostly short and too shallow, swift, or rock-filled to be of much use for transport. Coastal shipping was very important in linking major cities before railroads were built in the 1870s.

Exploring This Book

This book is divided into six chapters. This chapter is an introduction to early settlers on the Japanese islands. The next chapter discusses the influence of the Chinese on the Japanese lifestyle. Chapter 3 looks at the rule of the shoguns, while chapter 4 deals with the arrival of Europeans and the unification of Japan. Chapter 5 reveals the developing relationship between Japan and the West, and the final chapter looks at Japan today.

Japan was never successfully invaded until the American Occupation after World War II. America is now Japan's closest ally, and there are still U.S. forces with bases in Japan. Russia occupies some of the Kuril Islands, which Japan claims as its Northern Territories.

PACIFIC OCEAN

Mount Fuji is one of Japan's national symbols, and its highest mountain (12,388 feet; 3,776 meters high). It is an active volcano that has erupted 18 times in recorded history. The last time was in 1707. On a clear day it can be seen from a distance of 90 miles (150 kilometers.)

La Pérouse Strait

Sea of Okhotsk

Kuril Islands

HOKKAIDO

Daisetsu Mountains

Sapporo

Kushiro

Hakodate

Tsugaru Strait

Akita

Sado

Sendai

Niigata

Echigo Mountains

Sea of Japan

Utsunomiya

Kanazawa

HONSHU

Japan Alps

Izumo

Lake Biwa

Nagoya

Akaishi Mountains

Tokyo (Edo)

Yokohama

▲ Mt. Fuji

Kamakura

Kyoto (Heian-kyo)

Kobe

Miura

Okayama

Osaka

Shimoda

Hiroshima

Sakai

Nara

Oshima

Takamatsu

SHIKOKU

Kii Mountains

Kitakyushu

Fukuoka

KYUSHU

Nagasaki

▲ Mt. Kuju

Kyushu Mountains

Kagoshima

Korea Strait

Tsushima

Higashi Strait

Tanegashima Island

Osumi Island

Yakushima Strait

J A P A N

East China Sea

Sakashima Islands

Okinawa Islands

R y u k y u   I s l a n d s

Pacific Ocean

Early Settlers

The Japanese islands have been inhabited for at least 30,000 years. Fossil remains of plants and animals show that Japan was once joined to the mainland of Asia. The earliest inhabitants probably **migrated** along land bridges that once joined southern Honshu to Korea and Hokkaido to Siberia. What is now the Sea of Japan would have been a huge lake. About 20,000 years ago great **glaciers** melted, raising the level of the sea and creating the straits that separate Japan's main islands from each other and from the mainland.

From Hunters to Potters

The earliest inhabitants of Japan lived by hunting game and gathering wild plants. They used stone tools and weapons but did not make pottery until around 10,000 B.C. The invention of pottery made it possible to improve ways of cooking and storing food. The pattern used to decorate pots at that time is known as Jomon, which means "cord-marked." The centuries up to 300 B.C. are known as the Jomon period. Jomon people also made earthenware figures (*dogu*), which represented people or animals. Great piles of shells have been found at the sites of Jomon villages, showing that shellfish were an important part of their diet. Animal bones were used to make such things as needles and hairpins.

This clay figure, called a dogu, *dates from the fourth century B.C., at the end of the Jomon period.*

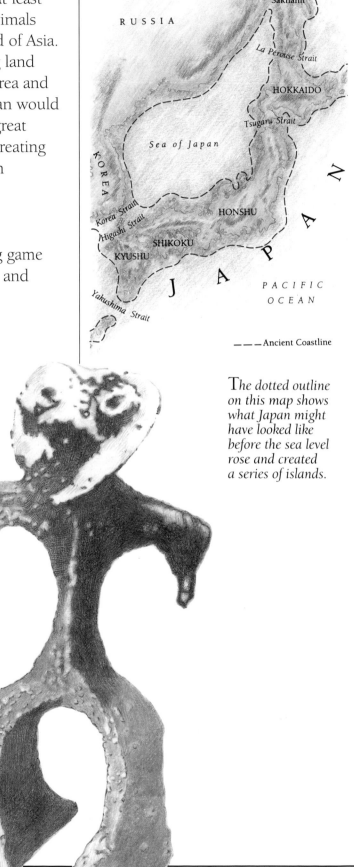

––– Ancient Coastline

The dotted outline on this map shows what Japan might have looked like before the sea level rose and created a series of islands.

The Ainu

One of the earliest groups of people to inhabit Japan were the Ainu. Most Japanese are descended from a mixture of **Mongol**, Malay, and Polynesian peoples. The Ainu are quite clearly different and more like the peoples of Siberia. They are taller, more heavily built, and have more facial and body hair than most Japanese. The Ainu language is quite different from Japanese, and very few people speak it today. In the Ainu language the word *ainu* simply means "man." In their religion the salmon, the owl, the killer whale, and the bear were especially sacred. Bears were sacrificed to carry messages to their ancestors.

Nowadays about 25,000 Ainu still live in Hokkaido. They carve wooden bears to sell to Japanese tourists, who visit reconstructed Ainu villages.

Exploring the Ainu

One of the first people to study the Ainu way of life was an Englishman, John Batchelor (1854–1944). Although he had no real education, he trained to become a **missionary** for the Church of England. In 1879 he came to Hokkaido to teach Christianity. To do this, he had to learn the Ainu language. By 1889 he was able to publish an Ainu-English-Japanese dictionary.

Batchelor built schools for the Ainu and gave them medical care. He lived among them for 60 years, until he was forced to leave when World War II broke out, in 1939.

This early photo of an Ainu man was taken about 100 years ago. Notice his bushy beard. He wears boots and warm clothing to protect himself against the chilly climate of Hokkaido.

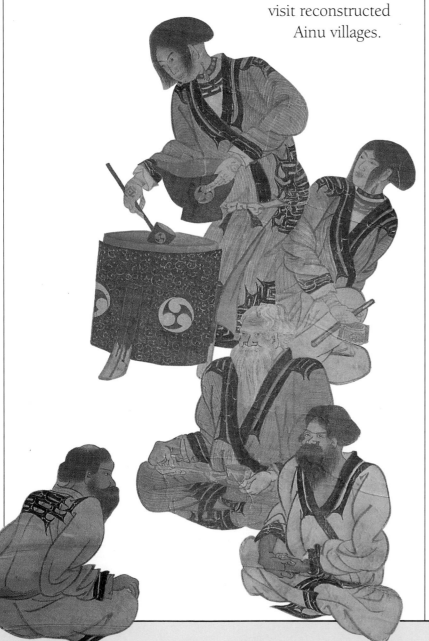

This detail from an 18th-century scroll shows an Ainu family. In that period only a few Japanese had any contact with the Ainu, who were regarded as primitive savages.

Rice and Emperors

The Japanese learned the skill of rice growing from the Chinese. These figures come from a Chinese painting. They are sorting the rice and transporting it.

This woman (below) is working in a flooded paddy field, transplanting rice seedlings by hand. Transplanting was traditionally women's work.

Between 300 B.C. and 300 A.D., the Japanese learned to grow rice, to work iron and bronze, and to weave cloth. These advances had come from China, probably brought by migrant peoples moving into Japan from Korea or Okinawa. This period is called the Yayoi period, after a village called Yayoicho. When the village was **excavated**, **archaeologists** found a new kind of pottery, smooth and painted, quite different from the Jomon. They also found that bronze – a mixture of tin and copper – had been used to make mirrors, bells, swords, and spears, and that iron had been used to make tools and farming implements.

Growing regular rice crops provided a more reliable food supply than hunting, so the population began to increase and people lived in larger villages. The leaders of the more powerful villages became chieftains, ruling over their neighbors. When they died, some were buried in mounds, which were separate from ordinary burial grounds, to show that they were important.

The First Emperor

Every ancient people had a creation myth, explaining how the world began. The Japanese believed that the world was created by gods who lived in heaven and that the sun goddess, Amaterasu, had given her grandson, Ninigi, a sword, a jewel, and a mirror and sent him to rule over Japan. According to Japan's oldest history books, written in 712 A.D. and 720 A.D., the first emperor, Jimmu, was Ninigi's grandson, who began his reign in 660 B.C. Japanese emperors are still given a sword, a jewel, and a mirror when they come to the throne.

The keyhole shaped tomb is said to have been built for the legendary emperor Nintoku around 400 A.D. It is nearly 1,640 feet (500 meters) long and surrounded by three moats. Building it would have involved as much labor as building one of the Egyptian pyramids.

This is a 19th-century colored wood-block print showing the sun goddess, Amaterasu Omikami. Her name means "great divinity illuminating heaven."

Haniwa clay figures, like this warrior, were placed around tombs as symbolic guards and servants.

The Tomb Builders

Modern historians think that Japan's line of emperors can be traced back to about 400 A.D., when a powerful family controlled an area of central Honshu called Yamato, which is the family name used by all emperors ever since. Between the 4th and 7th centuries, the Japanese buried their rulers and nobles in huge tombs (*kofun*) guarded by clay figures called haniwa (see right).

2 In the Shadow of China

Learning from China and Korea

A gagaku musician hitting a gong at the Shinto temple, Ise. Gagaku is an ancient form of court music in Japan.

The Japanese began to have direct contact with China around 400 A.D. China was much more powerful, wealthy, and advanced than Japan. The Japanese were very impressed and eagerly learned how to write, how to make porcelain, silk, **lacquer**, and paper, and how to lay out (plan) cities. They also took over the Chinese calendar and the **Buddhist** religion. For over 400 years Japan sent officials and scholars to China and in return welcomed many teachers, priests, and craftsworkers from there and Korea, who came to settle in Japan.

The Way of the Gods

The Japanese had their own religion, **Shinto**, which means "the way of the gods." It was based on the worship of nature and gods. Shinto had no great founder or prophet. It had no scriptures except myths that were eventually written down in the first Japanese books – the *Kojiki* and *Nihon shoki*. Shinto taught that every natural object, such as a lake or mountain, tree or rock, as well as any person, either living or dead, had a spirit (*kami*) that ought to be respected. Many Shinto festivals and celebrations began as ways of asking the gods to protect the rice crop or of thanking them for a good harvest.

The Great Buddha at Nara was built in the 8th century. It stands 53 feet (16.2 meters) high and is the world's largest statue of cast metal.

These are the Wedded Rocks at Futamigaura in Ise Bay. They are symbolic for Shinto followers, who believe that they sheltered the gods Izanagi and Izanami, the legendary creators of the islands of Japan.

Buddhism Comes to Japan

In 552 A.D. the king of Paekche in Korea sent some priests to the emperor of Japan with a statue of Buddha to explain the Buddhist religion. Buddha (**Enlightened** One) was the title given by his followers to an Indian teacher called Gautama. His teachings promised that if people lived a good, considerate, and unselfish life, they could escape being born over and over again, with all the pain, suffering, and illness that went with human life. The Buddha had died around 483 B.C., so Buddhism was already a thousand years old as a religion by the time it had spread through China and Korea to reach Japan.

Two Religions Side by Side

The Japanese were interested in Buddhism because it had a lot to teach about what happens to people when they die. Shinto was much more concerned about life in this world. So the two religions were thought to support each other. Japanese people came to believe that the Buddhist gods were Shinto spirits in another form. Nowadays most people still have a Shinto wedding and a Buddhist funeral.

An Age of Reform

Shotoku was a scholar who ruled as regent for Empress Suiko. His picture was used on Japanese banknotes until about five years ago.

Horyuji

The Horyuji Buddhist temple and monastery, near the ancient city of Nara, was first built in 607 by Prince Shotoku, a great patron of Buddhist learning. It burned down in 670, but was rebuilt immediately on an even larger scale and is now the oldest group of wooden buildings in the world. After his death, Shotoku was himself worshiped. Horyuji now has a great collection of 319 Buddhist art treasures and attracts thousands of visitors each year.

Prince Shotoku (574–622 A.D.) was interested in more than Buddhism. He also wanted to make the Japanese emperor as powerful in Japan as the Chinese emperor was in China. He introduced the Chinese idea of ruling through appointed officials rather than large landowners who could rebel against the emperor. Shotoku's plans were opposed by powerful courtiers, who thought they would lose their positions. A determined effort to put the plans into practice was made in 646 in a series of **reforms** known as Taika ("great change"). All land was declared to belong to the emperor.

Peasants were to pay **taxes** in rice or cloth or by working on building projects or serving as soldiers. To help the emperor extend his rule over the whole country, new roads were to be built and a postal service was established. A **census** of population was carried out in 670, so that the government could see how many taxpayers there were.

A Fixed Capital

Until the 7th century, the Japanese usually moved their capital every time an emperor died, because they thought it would be unlucky to stay in the same place. But gradually the emperors came to accept the Chinese idea of a fixed capital. One reason for a fixed capital was that it was very inconvenient to keep moving all the government records. In 710 the Japanese laid out a capital at Nara. It had a grid plan, like the Chinese capital Chang'an (Xian), the largest city in the world at that time, with a population of more than a million. By the middle of the century, Nara had a population of 200,000.

Horyuji's pagoda is the oldest in Japan. Pagodas were originally built over sacred relics associated with the Buddha. Horyuji became a famous center for the study of Buddhism.

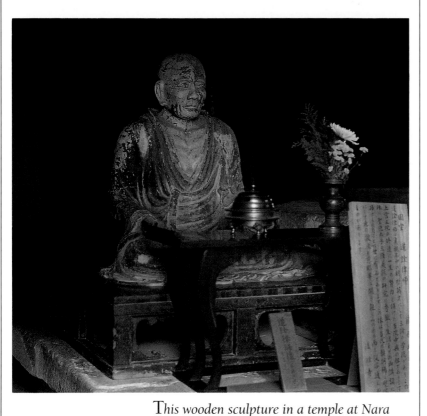

This wooden sculpture in a temple at Nara shows a Buddhist saint meditating with his legs crossed. Buddhist monks shaved their heads as a sign of poverty and to show they had no interest in worldly matters.

First Geography Books

In 713 the Japanese government ordered the **governor** of each **province** to send in a detailed written report describing the land, animals, plants, products, place-names, and legends of the area he was responsible for. The **survey** of land and resources was probably meant to help the government work out what taxes it could raise. The legends were written into the official history of the nation. Only 5 of the reports survive, more or less complete, although there were originally about 60.

An Emperors' Treasure House

The shosoin was built in 761 at Nara to store treasures belonging to the emperors. Made of cypress wood, it contains about 10,000 objects, including weapons, paintings, games, medicines, masks, pottery, and musical instruments. Some of the treasures were made as far away as Persia (modern-day Iran).

Capital of Peace and Tranquillity

This map shows the spread of Buddhist monasteries during the 7th and 8th centuries. The names on the map represent provinces that were formed during the Nara period.

Sea of Japan

HOKKAIDO

HAGURO

HOKURIKUDO
TOZANDO
TOKAIDO

HONSHU

SANINDO KINAI
SANYODO Heian-Kyo
Horyuji
Nara

NANKAIDO

SHIKOKU

SAIKAIDO
KYUSHU

Buddhism grew stronger throughout the Nara period, thanks to the support of the emperor and his courtiers. Buddhist monasteries were built in each province and received lands to support them. Buddhist leaders became so powerful that they began to interfere in politics. In 784 Emperor Kammu (737–806) decided that the best way to escape from their influence was to move the capital again. In 794 the capital settled at Heian-kyo, which means "capital of peace and tranquillity." Later this city came to be known as Kyoto. In theory it remained the capital of Japan until 1868, because emperors continued to live there. The years from 794 to 1185 are known as the Heian period.

Court and Countryside

The emperor and his courtiers lived a life of luxury, cut off from ordinary people. They dressed exquisitely. Courtiers passed the time composing poems and writing them in beautiful **calligraphy**. A great deal of detail is known about life at the Heian court thanks to books written by courtiers, such as *The Tale of Genji*, a novel written by

The Tale of Genji

This book tells the life of Prince Genji, who is called the shining prince because he is brilliant at everything he does – poetry, painting, dancing, music, and sport. Naturally he is also handsome and has beautiful manners. Although he has a successful career at court and is given many honors and gifts, he never really finds true happiness. Indirectly the story of Genji expresses the Buddhist idea that, in the end, human life is always sad. *The Tale of Genji* is a very long book, running to more than a thousand pages, with hundreds of different characters. It was written around 1000 A.D. and has been popular ever since.

Lady Murasaki Shikibu, and the diary kept by Sei Shonagon, another lady-in-waiting. Much less is known about the lives of the peasants, who made up 90 percent of the population – except that they worked hard and often suffered from plagues and attacks by bandits.

As the emperors preferred to pass their time studying or amusing themselves, the real power of appointing officials fell into the hands of court families, like the Fujiwara. They strengthened their hold on the emperors by marrying their daughters into the imperial family. Outside the capital itself, power was in the hands of large landowners. In theory, their land was a gift from the emperor and their titles meant that they were officials, appointed by the emperor. In practice, both lands and titles were often passed on within families. They increased their land by draining marshes and cutting down forests. They had their own private armies to force the peasants to work for them. So the Fujiwara also had to use bands of warriors to enforce the commands they made in the name of the emperor.

This is a statue of the monk Kukai dressed as a pilgrim. Kukai established the famous pilgrimage route, visiting 88 temples, in his home island of Shikoku.

Priests of the Shingon sect, which has 12,000 temples. Shingon teaches that everything is made from six elements – earth, water, fire, wind, space, and mind.

A Japanese Monk in China

In Japan the monk Kukai (774–835) is also known as Kobo Daishi (Great Teacher Kobo). In 804 he went with the official government mission to China to study Buddhism. But he was no ordinary student. He was an excellent poet, a brilliant calligrapher – and a fluent speaker of Chinese. When he went to Chang'an, the Chinese capital, the leading expert on Buddhism, Huiguo, welcomed him as a son. After two years Kukai returned to Japan and founded a monastery. In 823 the emperor invited him to become head of the most important monastery in Kyoto.

Japanese people believe that Kukai invented the *kana* system used in written Japanese (see page 4). He certainly compiled the oldest surviving Japanese dictionary. He also designed gardens and was a sculptor. Today the branch of Buddhism Kukai founded, Shingon (True Word), has 12 million followers.

3 Shoguns and Samurai

The Rise of the Samurai

As the emperor's government in Kyoto grew weaker, orders were still issued in his name, but they were often ignored outside the capital itself. The only taxes he could count on came from his own lands. The emperors, the Fujiwara family, and other courtiers all came to rely on bands of **samurai** warriors to support them.

A portrait (bottom left) of Yoritomo, the head of the Minamoto clan, painted by the artist Fujiwara no Takanobu on a silk scroll 800 years ago.

For the samurai (below), the bow was as important a weapon as the sword. Their armor was so light and flexible that they could swim in it.

The Heike Wars

In 1156 a quarrel broke out at court about who should be the next emperor. The two fighting sides were the Taira family, who had gained power by acting as leaders of the emperor's army, and the Minamoto family, who were supported by the Fujiwara. For a while the Taira, under Kiyomori, made themselves supreme at court and persuaded the emperor to give them titles and grants of land. But in 1180 they tried to make one of their newborn children emperor. This was going too far, and the Minamoto, led by the cunning Yoritomo (1147–99), saw their chance to strike back. In 1181 Kiyomori died of fever. Without their leader, the Taira were driven out of the capital by the Minamoto. The last great battle was fought at sea in 1185 at Dannoura, in the strait of Shimonoseki.

Tent Government

In 1192, Yoritomo persuaded the emperor to give him the title of **shogun**, which means "great barbarian-conquering supreme general." He established his permanent military headquarters at the coastal city of Kamakura because it was protected by mountains. For most of the next seven centuries, the real power in Japan was in the hands of shoguns, who gave orders in the name of the emperor. This system of ruling was known as the *bakufu* ("tent government") because generals gave orders from their tents when they were on campaign. Kamakura was now the real center of government, although, in theory, Kyoto was still the capital and the emperor was still the ruler.

Minamoto rule did not last long. Yoritomo was succeeded by his two sons, but after the second one was **assassinated** in 1219, power passed to the family of Yoritomo's wife. These were the Hojo – who were related to the Taira!

The Samurai

Samurai means "one who serves." Bushi means "fighting man." Bushi is usually used to describe the warriors of the period up to the 1800s. They lived on their own lands when they were not actually fighting. Warriors of the later period generally lived in castle towns and were paid in allowances of rice. They are referred to as samurai. These warriors were all expected to be fearless and loyal and to live plain, simple lives. They were expert horsemen and fought with swords, lances, and bows. They were willing to kill themselves on the battlefield rather than face giving themselves up. The proper name for this is *seppuku*, but it has become known among Westerners as *hara-kiri* (*belly slitting*).

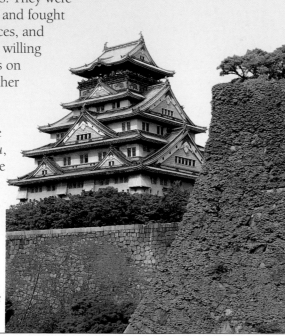

A *photograph of Osaka Castle (see also on page 24).*

Zen

A new kind of Buddhism became popular from the 12th century onward – Zen. Traditional Buddhism had encouraged believers to study scriptures based on Buddha's sermons or to take part in ceremonies of chanting or dancing. Zen, which began in China, developed another practice – meditation. Meditation meant learning to sit entirely still and calm, to clear the mind of worry and fear. Zen made its followers try to look beyond the obvious, whether they were dealing with people or problems.

Zen monks meditating.

Art Among the Ashes

There was another side to Japan during these years of warfare and disorder. Towns and markets grew. Trade with China began again. Merchants formed **guilds** to organize business better. The fact that many people had time to go on pilgrimages suggests that some were more prosperous, as does the interest in new arts such as gardening and flower arranging. Both these activities were strongly influenced by Zen, which encouraged people to see beauty in simple things.

Troubled Times

During the 13th century, China was conquered by the Mongols. The Mongol emperor **Kublai Khan** decided he wanted to conquer Japan as well. In 1274 and 1281 he sent huge fleets to invade it. Each time, the shogun gathered a great army to fight them off and spent a fortune building defenses along the coast. Each time, the Mongol fleets were scattered by typhoons.

A New Bakufu

The expense of fighting off the Mongols led to heavy taxes. Heavy taxes led to rebellions. The Hojo family became more and more unpopular as government finances slid into chaos. The emperor Go-Daigo saw a chance to take power back into his own hands and in 1333 raised an army to challenge the Hojo. The Hojos sent a general called Ashikaga Takauji (1305–58) to put down the emperor's uprising. Instead he joined the emperor's side. When they marched on the Hojos' headquarters, the Hojo all committed suicide.

This print shows the Japanese monk Nichiren surrounded by Mongol warriors. Nichiren gained great influence when he correctly predicted that the Mongols would try to conquer Japan.

Go-Daigo soon made himself as unpopular as the Hojos. He gave all the most important jobs and estates to his courtiers and ignored the samurai generals who had put him back in power. In 1336 Ashikaga Takauji led a rebellion against Go-Daigo and forced him to flee to Yoshino, in the mountains south of Nara. From then until 1392 there were two imperial courts – a southern court at Yoshino and a northern one in Kyoto that gave the title of shogun to the Ashikaga family.

An Age of Chaos

In 1466 a quarrel broke out in the Ashikaga family over who was to be the next shogun. The outcome was the Onin war (1467–77), which reduced most of Kyoto to ashes. The Ashikaga became just one more warlord family among dozens of others, although they kept the title of shogun until 1588. For more than a century, Japan was divided among ambitious soldiers. The most important warlords were called **daimyo**, which means "great name."

With no strong central government to suppress them, the country was plagued by bandits and pirates. In the middle of all this chaos – and quite by accident – Japan suddenly made contact for the first time with Europeans.

No Drama

No is a kind of drama that began in 4th-century Kyoto. The actors were all men. They had gorgeous costumes, and some wore masks. There was no scenery, except a painted background, but there were musicians who accompanied the actors as they chanted words and moved slowly. The stories for No plays often came from Buddhism. Troupes of No actors were employed by temples and shrines and performed at religious festivals. No is still performed by professional actors.

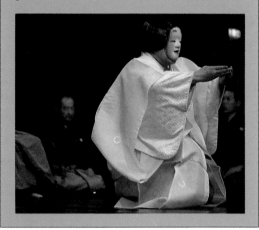

The Tea Ceremony

Tea was introduced to Japan from China in the Nara period and at first it was used as a medicine. The monk Eisai (1141–1215) is said to have brought tea seeds back with him in 1191 after visiting China. He and other monks believed that tea kept them alert while meditating. To fit the calm mood of meditation, participants would prepare the tea in a slow, careful manner. Gradually the custom of preparing and drinking tea in quiet and tasteful surroundings spread to aristocrats and merchants. The greatest master of the tea ceremony (*chanoyu*) was a merchant, Sen-No Rikyu (1522–91). He believed that the most important part of the tea ceremony was not the implements people used but the mood of relaxed appreciation they created. The tea ceremony remains extremely popular in Japan to this day.

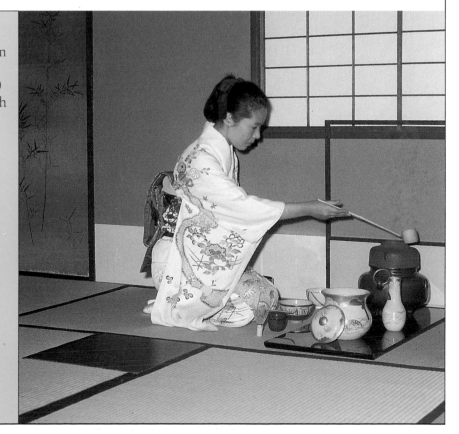

4 The Coming of the Barbarians

Guns and Missionaries

The first Europeans to reach Japan were two Portuguese passengers aboard a Chinese **junk** that had to land at Tanegashima Island, off Kyushu, to make repairs after a storm. This happened in 1543. The Portuguese at that time had a great fleet which was trying to control the highly profitable Asian spice trade. They had "factories" (trading posts) from India to China. After their accidental contact with Japan, the Portuguese soon went back to find out what Japan had to offer.

The Japanese were certainly eager to trade for one thing – guns. They knew about gunpowder from the Chinese, who used it for making fireworks and signal rockets. But before the arrival of the Portuguese, the Japanese had never seen a gun. Within six months of seeing one, Japanese **armorers** had learned how to make them.

The arrival of the Portuguese started a craze for imported novelties from Europe, such as clocks. Europeans also introduced products from other areas of the world such as carpets from the Middle East, tobacco from America, and sweet potatoes from the Philippines.

The warlord Oda Nobunaga (right) began the task of reuniting Japan. He is holding an iron fan for giving signals to troops on the battlefield. Oda was ambushed and killed during a tea ceremony.

The warlord Oda Nobunaga managed to unite about a third of Japan.

A Revolution in Warfare

One of the first people to understand the importance of guns was the warlord Oda Nobunaga (1534–82). As early as 1549 he organized an infantry unit of 500 men, all armed with guns. His ambition was to put "all the country under one sword" – his! Soon after guns came cannons, which again changed the nature of warfare.

In 1569 Oda captured the port of Sakai, an important center for manufacturing guns and cannons. In 1575 he won a victory over his rivals at Nagashino, where he gathered 3,000 musketeers to wipe out a huge cavalry charge. By the time of his death, Oda had managed to bring a third of the country under his control.

Jesuit Missionaries

In 1549, **Jesuit** missionaries, led by Francis Xavier, landed in Japan to **convert** the people to Christianity. There was no strong government to forbid them, but there was the problem of the Japanese language. The Jesuits found it so difficult that they said it must have been invented by the devil to stop them from spreading their religion. In 1603–04 they finally printed a Portuguese-Japanese dictionary, with 33,000 entries.

Southern Barbarians

The Japanese called the newcomers *namban*, which means "southern barbarians," because they came to Japan from the south. All Japanese have black hair, so they were fascinated by the Portuguese, with brown or blond hair. They were amazed by the dark skins of Indian and Indonesian sailors on Portuguese ships. The pictures they painted show that the Japanese thought the strangers' baggy trousers were odd and their pointed noses even odder!

Japan Unified

In 1582 Oda Nobunaga was assassinated by one of his own generals. He was soon revenged by another of his commanders, Toyotomi Hideyoshi (1536–98), an ugly little man whom Oda had nicknamed Monkey. But Toyotomi was a superb general. By 1587 he had added the southern island of Kyushu to Oda's conquests. Three years later he controlled eastern Japan as well.

Toyotomi was determined to bring the civil wars to an end for good, so he ordered all peasants to give up their weapons and go back to farming. Samurai were ordered out of villages and told to live in castle towns, where they could be controlled by the daimyo, who paid them. Toyotomi also ordered a detailed land survey and census so that he could set up an efficient tax system and work out how many samurai he could feed. His tax system lasted for the next 300 years. Peasants were guaranteed the right to work their land – at the price of being forbidden to leave it.

The sword is the soul of the samurai.

Conquering the World?

After he had united Japan, Toyotomi decided to attack Korea. In 1592 he sent 150,000 Japanese troops to Korea. The Koreans fought back, with Chinese support. The fighting was very savage and caused immense suffering. Gradually the Japanese were forced back. In 1598, as he was nearing death, Toyotomi ordered the Japanese to withdraw from Korea.

Toyotomi wanted to make sure that his lands went to his baby son, Hideyori. So he set up a **council** of five daimyo to make sure this happened. One of them was Tokugawa Ieyasu (1543–1616), his most trusted ally.

A Journey to Rome

By 1580, six daimyo had become Christians, possibly because they hoped to profit from trading with the Portuguese. Because they had converted, so had their samurai and servants. Now there were about 100,000 Japanese Christians. In 1582, four Japanese Christian boys were sent to Europe, where they were welcomed by Philip II of Spain and Pope Gregory XIII. They returned to Japan in 1590, and all four joined the Jesuit order.

This picture of Toyotomi makes him look calm and dignified. In fact, he was a coarse and ill-mannered man, with a ferocious temper.

The invasion into Korea led by Toyotomi Hideyoshi.

Ieyasu was cool and calculating. The dynasty he founded ruled Japan for over 250 years.

Back to Front

The missionaries found many Japanese customs very strange and often just the opposite of the way things were in Europe. A Jesuit called Luis Frois made a list of them, in the first history of Japan written by a Westerner. He noticed that Japanese people preferred fish to meat and often ate fish raw, whereas Europeans would only eat fish cooked. Japanese people **cremated** their dead, rather than burying them. Even the way they wrote their books was the opposite of the European way. The Japanese wrote from top to bottom rather than side to side and right to left, not left to right – which meant that, to Europeans, their books opened at the back, not the front!

The Last Bakufu

Ieyasu soon broke his promise to see that Hideyori inherited power. In 1600 he defeated Hideyori's supporters at the battle of Sekigahara, although Hideyori himself lived on. In 1603 Ieyasu asked the emperor to make him shogun. Ieyasu's family, the Tokugawa, were to rule as shoguns until 1868. Their bakufu headquarters at Edo became the real center of power, just as Kamakura had (see page 17), although Kyoto was still, in theory, the capital. But unlike Kamakura, Edo grew to become Japan's biggest city. By 1750 it had a population of more than a million and was probably the largest city in the world.

In 1614 Ieyasu surrounded Hideyori's stronghold at Osaka Castle and tricked him into filling in the moat. In 1615 the castle was taken and Hideyori killed himself. Ieyasu died the following year, having already passed on the title of shogun to his son.

The siege of Osaka Castle caused huge damage, but the castle was rebuilt in 1620. Once Ieyasu had taken this last enemy stronghold, the power of the Tokugawa dynasty was finally secure. This painting is a detail from a folding screen.

This picture shows William Adams in 1600 talking to Ieyasu about a model of a European-style ship.

The Shogun's Englishman

William Adams (1564–1620) is the only foreigner ever to have been made a samurai. He came to Japan in 1600 as the pilot of a crippled Dutch ship that **beached** on Kyushu. The warlord Ieyasu questioned Adams, who told him a lot about European shipping and warfare. So Ieyasu ordered Adams to teach his men about gunnery and map making. He also instructed him to build two European-style ships. For this reason the Japanese regard Adams as the founder of their navy.

Ieyasu refused to let Adams go back to England but gave him an estate at Miura. Adams married the daughter of a Japanese official and had two children. He admired the Japanese and wrote that they were "good of nature, courteous above measure and valiant in war." The Japanese call him Miura Anjin – the pilot of Miura – and hold a ceremony in his honor every year at his grave.

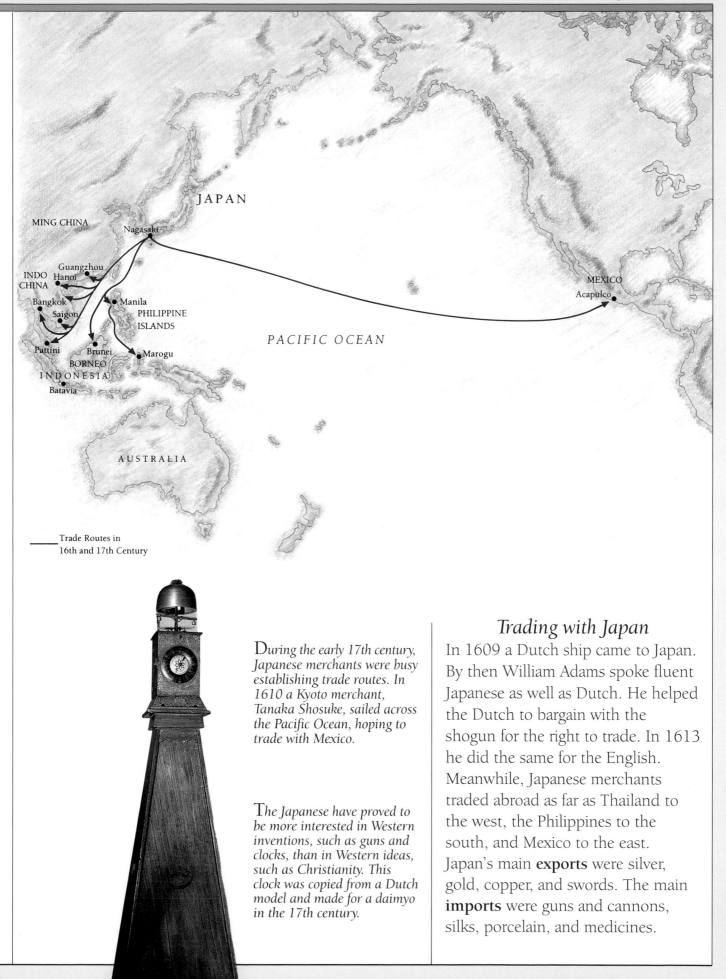

MING CHINA

Nagasaki

JAPAN

Guangzhou
INDO   Hanoi
CHINA

Bangkok

Saigon

Manila

PHILIPPINE
ISLANDS

Pattini

Brunei

Marogu

BORNEO

INDONESIA

Batavia

PACIFIC OCEAN

MEXICO
Acapulco

AUSTRALIA

Trade Routes in
16th and 17th Century

During the early 17th century, Japanese merchants were busy establishing trade routes. In 1610 a Kyoto merchant, Tanaka Shosuke, sailed across the Pacific Ocean, hoping to trade with Mexico.

The Japanese have proved to be more interested in Western inventions, such as guns and clocks, than in Western ideas, such as Christianity. This clock was copied from a Dutch model and made for a daimyo in the 17th century.

Trading with Japan

In 1609 a Dutch ship came to Japan. By then William Adams spoke fluent Japanese as well as Dutch. He helped the Dutch to bargain with the shogun for the right to trade. In 1613 he did the same for the English. Meanwhile, Japanese merchants traded abroad as far as Thailand to the west, the Philippines to the south, and Mexico to the east. Japan's main **exports** were silver, gold, copper, and swords. The main **imports** were guns and cannons, silks, porcelain, and medicines.

25

Closing the Country

The crucifixion of 26 martyrs at Nagasaki in 1597 marked the beginning of religious persecution.

So long as there was no strong government in Japan, the Jesuits were free to preach. But as soon as Toyotomi Hideyoshi (see pages 22-23) had conquered Kyushu, where the Christians were most numerous, he began to **persecute** them. In 1597 he ordered 26 Christians, including 9 European missionaries, to be crucified at Nagasaki. The Japanese government became increasingly worried that one of the Christian daimyo might try to start another war and bring in foreign troops.

But Ieyasu thought that foreigners could be useful and kept them in their place by playing one off against another. His son, Hidetada, thought that Japan would be better off without them and cut down the trading rights of the English. Soon after Adams died, the English closed their factory and left Japan.

Eyewitness for a Century

German-born Engelbert Kaempfer (1651–1716) qualified as a doctor before joining a Swedish **embassy** to Persia in 1683. From there he traveled through Thailand and Indonesia and reached Japan in 1690, where he worked as the doctor for the Dutch settlement at Dejima. In 1691 and 1692 Kaempfer joined the annual expedition to Edo to give presents to the shogun. This gave him a rare chance to see what Japan was like. He returned to Europe in 1693, smuggling out a collection of Japanese books and maps. Thirty-five years later, a two-volume *History of Japan* (1727–28), based on his collection of Japanese materials and his experiences, was published. It appeared in Dutch, French, and German editions and remained the standard European work on Japan for over a century.

A "hundred things shop" (department store) in 17th-century Edo.

When a new shogun, Iemitsu, came to power in 1623, he celebrated by having 50 Christians killed. Between 1633 and 1639, his government issued a series of laws. These forbade the Japanese to go abroad or, if they were abroad, forbade them to return on pain of death. They forbade the building of oceangoing ships, banned Christianity, and limited foreign trade to the Dutch and Chinese.

The Dutch at Dejima

In 1641 the Dutch were ordered to move their trading post to Dejima, an artificial island in Nagasaki Harbor, paid for by 25 wealthy Japanese merchants who benefited from overseas trade. This tiny patch of land was to be the only place foreigners were allowed to live in Japan until 1854. No other Europeans were allowed to trade with Japan at all. As far as the Japanese were concerned, foreign trade was a luxury, not a necessity.

A Dutch sailing ship with flags flying.

Japanese often like to use short poems as pieces of calligraphy and accompany them with sketches. The aim is to use a few words and brush strokes to suggest much more than is said or shown.

A Poet on the Move

Matsuo Basho (1644–94) is known to all Japanese as the great master of haiku, a form of short poem that has three lines of five, seven, and five syllables. Haiku are like snapshots that record a single moment or feeling rather than tell a story.

Basho became a popular teacher of haiku in Edo and lived well. But success made him feel that he was becoming lazy. For the last ten years of his life, he took to traveling in the hope that seeing nature firsthand would help him write better poetry. Basho wrote accounts of his travels that were a mixture of diary, poems, and descriptions of places he had seen.

Basho's greatest journey took him to the remotest parts of Honshu, over the mountains and along the Japan Sea coast, covering 1,440 miles (2,400 kilometers) in 156 days. His account of this, *The Narrow Road to the Deep North,* was published in the year of his death. It shows how much the poet was moved by the beauty of Japan's landscape and its history.

Know Your Place!

The ideas of Confucius governed Japanese society during the period of Tokugawa rule. All educated samurai read his writings.

The main aim of the Tokugawa government (1603–1868) was peace. They controlled about a quarter of all the land, and around their own holdings they created barrier lands held by their most trusted followers (*fudai*), daimyo who had fought on their side at Sekigahara (see page 24). Their former enemies were treated as "outer lords" (*tozama*) and left to rule estates on the fringes of the country. Spies and informers were used to guard against unauthorized **fortifications** or marriage alliances between powerful families.

A Confucian Society

The Tokugawa government supported the ideas of the ancient Chinese scholar **Confucius** (551–479 B.C.), who thought disorder was the greatest evil and praised loyalty and obedience. Samurai were at the top of society because they ruled. Next came farmers, who produced food, then craftspeople, who created things. Merchants came below craftspeople, because they didn't make anything. Scholars, doctors and priests were on the same level as samurai, because they usually came from samurai families and were educated. Women were always supposed to obey men.

Strengths and Weaknesses

That was the theory. In practice, peace enabled trade to prosper, and many merchants became very wealthy. As samurai borrowed money from them, the merchants used their debts to gain power over them. Peasants didn't always put up with their hard life, and there were more than 2,000 revolts during Tokugawa times. One reason for this was that without foreign trade, Japan was running out of food. A series of bad harvests in the 1780s and 1830s led to famines and epidemics.

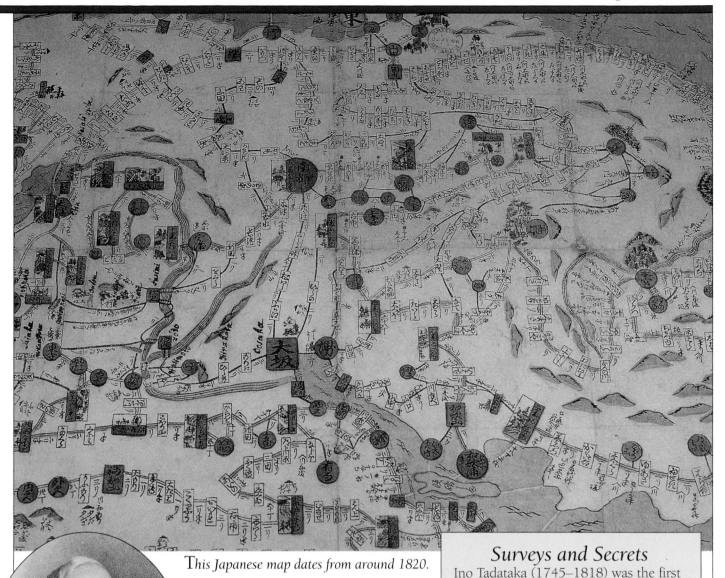

This Japanese map dates from around 1820.

The Study of Japan

The founder of the study of Japan was the German Philipp Franz von Siebold (1796–1866). Like Kaempfer, he was employed by the Dutch East India Company as a doctor for the trading post at Dejima, where he arrived in 1823. A year later he set up a college where he taught Western medicine to the Japanese in return for their reports on Japan and its people. One of von Siebold's pupils, Ito Gemboku (1800–71), went on to pioneer **vaccination** against smallpox in Japan. The center he set up for this became Tokyo University's School of Medicine.

Philipp von Siebold

Ito Gemboku

Surveys and Secrets

Ino Tadataka (1745–1818) was the first person to produce a complete survey of Japan using Western scientific methods – and he didn't start it until he was nearly 50. Ino studied with the shogun's official astronomer, Takahashi Yoshitoki, who had some Dutch books about astronomy and surveying.

By the time he was 70, Ino had spent 3,737 days on the road, taking measurements, and had walked 26,220 miles (43,700 kilometers). Ino died in 1818, but his death was kept secret by his devoted **disciples**. In 1821 his great work was finished and published by Takahashi Kageyasu, who had followed his father as official astronomer. Takahashi also added information about the northern islands of Hokkaido and Sakhalin. Ino's maps were still in use 100 years after his death.

5 Opening Up

Intrusion and Revolution

In 1846 the American government decided that it was time Japan opened up to foreigners. In July 1853 four American warships anchored off Edo. Their commander, Commodore Matthew Perry, delivered a message asking for trading rights and promising to return the following year for an answer. In February 1854 he came back with eight ships. They brought many gifts, including a miniature railroad with 328 feet (100 meters) of track. They also gave demonstrations of military **drill**. The message was fairly clear. Agree – or else!

The shogun's government agreed to sign a **treaty** that allowed American ships to visit the ports of Shimoda and Hakodate to buy supplies and offer fair treatment to shipwrecked sailors. The treaty also allowed the Americans to have a **consul** living at Shimoda to look after American interests. By 1856 Britain, France, Russia, and the Netherlands all had similar treaties. In 1858 the shogun's government agreed to open more ports and gave the foreigners further rights. Many samurai found these "unequal treaties" bitterly humiliating.

These three prints depict London, painted by a Japanese artist who had never seen it. Notice the warships and soldiers, showing Britain as a warlike country.

A *contemporary Japanese print showing one of Commodore Perry's ships in Edo Bay.*

The Meiji Restoration

Japan was deeply divided by the coming of the Westerners. Many samurai wanted to drive them back into the sea.

Japan's crisis was settled by a brief civil war, in 1867–68. Led by the Choshu and Satsuma clans, an army of samurai overthrew the Tokugawa. To make it clear that this was in the best interests of Japan, they claimed they were restoring power to where it rightly belonged – with the emperor. In Japan emperors choose a name for their reign (*nengo*), and the teenage emperor decided to call his reign Meiji, which means "Enlightened Rule." The emperor moved from Kyoto to Edo – which then became Tokyo, or "Eastern Capital."

The Iwakura Mission

In 1871 a high-level mission of 50 **diplomats**, experts, and interpreters was sent to the West to see whether the "unequal treaties" signed by the shogun's government

could be revised. Attempts to rewrite the treaties were dropped after the United States proved unwilling to do so. So the mission concentrated on visiting factories, schools, hospitals, and other institutions to see how they worked and how Japan might benefit from Western technology and institutions. The group returned home determined to enrich the country and strengthen the army. By then, Japan's modernization was well under way.

Even before the return of the Iwakura mission, great changes were taking place. After its return, they happened even faster. In 1870 Tokyo and the new port of Yokohama were linked by telegraph, and a railroad between the two was opened in 1872. In 1876 samurai were forbidden to wear swords. The first Japanese newspaper was published in 1871. In 1872 the first modern census showed that Japan had a population of 33,110,825. The Western calendar was adopted in 1873, the same year in which the emperor and empress started to wear Western-style dress rather than traditional Japanese costumes.

Enough!

For many Japanese these changes were going too far, too fast. In 1874 there was a rebellion by discontented samurai. In 1876 there were three more rebellions. The last and greatest was led by a hero of the civil war that had put the modernizing government in power – Saigo Takamori (1827–77). His army of 40,000 samurai was beaten by the new army of peasant **conscripts** in Western-style uniforms. He committed suicide on the battlefield.

Saigo's defeat did not mean the end of the samurai, although they did lose their privileges. Only a few could become officers in the new army. Others became policemen, postmasters, or railroad officials. Thousands became teachers. They instructed their pupils to behave as they had been taught – to be brave, loyal, and hardworking.

Saigo Takamori – a samurai rebel against too much change.

Civilization and Enlightenment

The craze for Western things reached its height in the 1880s. Japan's rulers seemed convinced that Western countries were the source of every kind of "civilization and enlightenment." In 1883 the government opened the Rokumeikan (Pavilion of the Deer's Cry), a Western-style building where Japanese – in Western dress – could meet foreigners to dance, listen to concerts, play cards, and raise money for charities. Japanese writers began to compose poems and novels in the Western style. In 1889 the emperor granted a **constitution** with an elected parliament, called the National Diet.

Japan's Leading Westernizer

Fukuzawa Yukichi (1835–1901) learned Dutch when he was 20. When he discovered that Holland was then, politically, a much less important country than Britain or America, he immediately began to learn English. In 1860 he went with the first Japanese mission to America and in 1862 traveled with the first mission to Europe. In 1867 he began to publish a ten-volume series called *Conditions in the West*. The first volume sold 150,000 copies. But Fukuzawa was not popular with everyone. For over ten years he was unable to go out at night for fear of being murdered by samurai who opposed Westernization.

Young Fukuzawa, wearing the sword of the samurai.

Japan's National Diet and constitution were based on that of Germany – another country led by an emperor and determined to become a great modern power. The National Diet building dates from the 1930s and is a symbol of the new constitution.

This photo was taken in the 19th century and shows Japanese country life as it was then. Little had changed for many years, since most of the developments were happening in the cities and among court and government officials.

Fukuzawa continued to write and spread his ideas by founding a newspaper and a leading university, Keio. He was in favor of women's rights and believed that among the things the new Japan needed most were people who were completely free and unafraid to speak out.

Keep Japan Japanese!

The geographer Shiga Shigetaka (1863–1927) grew up at the height of the craze for Western things. In 1886 he traveled through the South Pacific. Everywhere he saw that the local people were doing all the hard work while the Westerners grew rich. When he came home, he wrote *Conditions in the South Seas* to warn Japanese people against the danger of falling under Western control.

In 1888 Shiga helped to found the Society for Political Education to spread this message, to oppose the "unequal treaties," to campaign against pollution, and to support Japanese acquisition of its own colonies overseas. He became a lecturer in geography at Waseda University. In 1894 he published a book about Japan's landscape, which created much public interest in mountaineering and led to his appointment as head of the Forestry Bureau at the Ministry of Agriculture. Britain recognized his work by making him an honorary Fellow of the Royal Geographical Society.

Change and Old Ways

The 1880s were the high point of the craze for change. However, the different attitudes that Japanese had toward change can be seen in the contrasting careers of Ito Hirobumi (1841–1909) and Itagaki Taisuke (1837–1919). Both men took part in the wars that overthrew the Tokugawa bakufu and served as ministers in the new government that was modernizing Japan. Itagaki took a leading part in calling for a parliament and founded Japan's first modern political party. He spent much of his later career criticizing the

The Japanese parliament was formed by those who overthrew the Tokugawa bakufu.

government. Ito was the man who wrote the constitution that gave Japan a parliament. He served four times as prime minister but was suspicious of party politics and believed that political leaders should think of themselves as servants of the emperor.

Live Machines

The rush to modernize meant that Japan had to import foreign experts as teachers, technicians, and advisers. They were addressed as "Honorable Foreign Expert," but behind their backs they were sometimes referred to as "live machines." The Japanese employed more than 4,000 of them, about half of them British. The Japanese chose their experts very carefully. The British were selected for their knowledge of navigation, shipbuilding, railroads, lighthouses, steelmaking, and drains. French and Germans were employed as soldiers, doctors, and experts on local government. Americans were hired as experts on education and agriculture. The Japanese were determined to learn from foreigners, not to rely on them.

Ito Hirobumi believed that political leaders should be loyal to the emperor.

America's "Japan Man"

W. E. Griffis (1843–1928) was in Japan for less than four years, but his 18 books and hundreds of magazine articles about the country made him recognized as America's leading expert. He saw at first hand how quickly the country had changed from disorder and poverty to a wealthy industrialized nation. He also realized that "the Japanese simply want helpers and advisers. They propose to keep the 'bossing'… and all the power in their own hands." Within two years after returning home, he published *The Mikado's Empire*, which had been reprinted 12 times by 1913. The Japanese government twice honored him with the Order of the Rising Sun, an official decoration to recognize his services to Japan.

Japan on the move! Wheeled vehicles, railroads, and oceangoing ships were all new to Japan. They speeded up communications and put Japan in touch with the wider world.

Things Japanese

The British equivalent of Griffis was Basil Hall Chamberlain (1850–1935), whose humorous dictionary *Things Japanese* (1890) went through six editions. By the time he left Japan in 1911, he had risen from instructor in English at the navy school to become the first professor of Japanese at Tokyo University, where he pioneered the study of early Japanese history, poetry, and language.

Rescuing the Past

What Chamberlain did for literature, two Americans did for archaeology and art. Edward S. Morse (1838–1925) came to Japan in 1877 to teach zoology, but as soon as he arrived, he also conducted Japan's first archaeological dig, at Omori. Before he left in 1880, he helped to found Japan's first modern museum. In 1886 he published *Japanese Homes and Their Surroundings*, which introduced Western readers to Japanese architecture.

Ernest Fenellosa (1853–1908) was invited to Japan to teach **economics**, but he soon became a passionate defender of traditional Japanese art. Fenellosa used his position at the Ministry of Education to reintroduce Japanese-style art lessons in school and to persuade the government to control the export of works of art. He also helped to found the college that became the Tokyo University of Fine Arts and Music and wrote books about Japanese wood-block prints and traditional No drama (see page 19).

Globe-Trotters

Sir Rutherford Alcock

Britain's first diplomat in Japan was Sir Rutherford Alcock (1809–97). In 1863 Alcock published an account of his time in Japan, *The Capital of the Tycoon*. Like Frois (see page 23), he portrayed it as a topsy-turvy land in which everything seemed to be the wrong way around. "There old men fly kites while the children look on; the carpenter uses his plane by drawing it to him and their tailors stitch from them; they mount their horses from the off-side – the horses stand in the stables with their heads where we place their tails . . . ladies black their teeth instead of keeping them white." And as for men and women mixing together naked in the public bathhouses . . . words failed him. What serious traveler could resist such a fascinating country?

Gilbert and Sullivan's comic opera The Mikado *took advantage of Britain's 1880s craze for Japanese things. The authentic costumes were supplied by Libertys of Regent Street, London, which specialized in importing real Japanese silks and fans.*

Unbeaten Tracks in Japan

Isabella Bird (1831–1904) certainly couldn't resist the challenge of Japan and found her 1,380-mile (2,300 kilometer) horseback trek through northern Honshu and Hokkaido thoroughly worth the effort: "Japan offers as much novelty perhaps as an excursion to another planet." But she didn't always like or approve of what she saw: "The Japanese are the most irreligious people that I have ever seen – their pilgrimages are picnics, and their religious festivals fairs."

Isabella Bird

Dolls' Houses

In 1889 the writer Rudyard Kipling stopped off in Japan on his way from India to England. The contrast with India was striking: "It is strange to be in a clean land and stranger to walk among dolls' houses. It would pay us to . . . take away any fear of invasion . . . and pay the country as much as ever it chose, on condition that it simply sat still and went on making beautiful things."

Japonisme

Japan's biggest impact on Westerners was in the field of art. European artists were fascinated by the brightly colored wood-block prints (*ukiyo-e*) produced by artists such as Hokusai (1760–1849) and Hiroshige (1797–1858). The prints first came to Europe as packaging wrapped round porcelain bowls and vases. More than a hundred were exhibited at the 1867 Paris *Exposition Universelle*. French artists, such as Claude Monet and Edgar Degas, were keen collectors. The French art critic Burty called the craze Japonisme. In Britain the fashion was spread by the American artist James Whistler. His paintings show not only woodblock prints but also Japanese vases and flower arrangements, and models wearing **kimono** and holding Japanese fans.

This painting of dancers by Edgar Degas was influenced by Japanese art.

First Impressions

Lafcadio Hearn (1850–1904) was an Irish-Greek who lived in America and the West Indies before landing in Japan in 1890. He was absolutely enchanted and wrote in an excited essay called "My First Day in the Orient": "Everything Japanese is delicate, exquisite, admirable – even a pair of common wooden chopsticks in a paper bag with a little drawing on it. The bank bills, the commonest copper coins are things of beauty. Even the piece of plaited colored string used by the shopkeeper in tying up your last purchase is a pretty curiosity." Hearn never left Japan. He married a Japanese and became a Japanese citizen in 1896, taking the name Koizumi Yakumo. He became an expert on Japanese legends and customs.

Photographing Japan

If there was ever a really serious visitor it was Herbert G. Ponting, a Fellow of the Royal Geographical Society, who spent three years in Japan so that he could "photograph the country to my heart's content." The result was a book of nearly 400 pages, *In Lotus Land* (1909). Photography wasn't always easy. In Kyoto he was moved on by the police when he tried to take a picture of a holy procession. At Osaka Castle he was arrested by the army, who thought he was a Russian spy. The first time he tried to take views of the inside of a volcanic crater, he was dismayed to find that the sulfurous fumes ruined his photographic plates.

Herbert Ponting trying to photograph a volcano. Some aspects of "old Japan" were recorded by Western photographers just before the scenes disappeared forever.

Alliance and Defiance

The late 19th and early 20th centuries were dominated by war with other countries. In the 1880s Japanese generals became very concerned about Korea, a weak and backward kingdom that was also the nearest part of Asia to Japan. Both China and Japan interfered in Korean politics. In 1894 they went to war over who was to control Korea. Japanese forces, although outnumbered, won easily. The Chinese island of Formosa (Taiwan) was handed over and became a Japanese colony.

Japan fought twice to gain control of Korea, which it called "a dagger point at the heart of Japan" (left).

A popular print of the naval battle of 1905 in the Sea of Japan, where Admiral Togo defeated the Russians (above).

War with Russia

In 1904–05 Japan fought Russia over Korea and won again, though it was a much harder fight. Japan gained the southern half of Sakhalin (see page 29). In 1910 Korea became a Japanese colony. The Koreans resisted but were crushed. In Taiwan, by contrast, Japan helped improve conditions by building roads, schools, and hospitals and encouraging better farming methods.

By 1911 all the Western powers had agreed to abolish the "unequal treaties" signed back in the 1850s. Many Japanese drew the conclusion that aggression was the best way for a nation to earn respect.

A postcard drawn in 1905 showing Japanese supremacy over the Russians.

The Road to War

During World War I, Japan fought on the Allied side. In 1919 at the Paris Peace Conference, Japan was treated as one of five great powers. The conference formed a new League of Nations, to settle international disputes. However, the collapse of world trade between 1929 and 1931 led to political crises in every major country. In Japan there was mass unemployment. Junior officers in the army demanded that Japan enlarge her Asian empire by force as a way of solving the nation's problems. Politicians who opposed this policy were murdered.

In 1931, Japanese forces in Asia invaded the Chinese province of Manchuria. The government in Tokyo was too weak to stop them. In 1932 a **puppet state** of Manchukuo was set up, with real power in Japanese hands.

A Japanese woodblock print shows Japanese Red Cross nurses helping the wounded in the Sino-Japanese war.

In 1923 an earthquake hit Tokyo, adding to Japan's troubles.

Japan at War

Allied Countries

Axis Countries

Axis then Allied

Neutral

The map above shows the various alliances of countries during the Second World War.

Below is a print of the Japanese surprise air attack on Pearl Harbor, Hawaii, on December 7, 1941.

When the League of Nations condemned the invasion of China, Japan left the League and in 1936 allied itself with the other warlike powers, Germany and Italy.

In 1937 an all-out invasion of China was launched. The United States tried to force Japan to pull back by cutting off supplies of steel and then oil. Believing that war with the United States was unavoidable, Japan launched a surprise attack on the U.S. naval base at Pearl Harbor, Hawaii, on December 7, 1941.

Victory and Defeat

For six months after Pearl Harbor, the Japanese forces seemed unstoppable, taking Hong Kong and then, in February 1942, Singapore, the main British base in eastern Asia. Soon they threatened the borders of India. But the great naval battles of the Coral Sea and Midway Island in the summer of 1942 destroyed the Japanese navy's striking power. The Allies (U.S., Britain, and U.S.S.R.) were free to strike back, re-taking Pacific islands until they could establish bases from which Japan could be attacked and bombed.

A three-day raid on Tokyo in March 1945 killed more than 100,000 people. The Japanese prepared to resist the invasion of their homeland. Young pilots volunteered for suicide missions against Allied shipping. Two thousand planes flew in these attacks, sinking 34 ships and damaging 288 more. In defending the island of Okinawa, the Japanese lost 100,000 soldiers and 150,000 civilians, many in mass suicides of schoolchildren and nurses.

Japan's eventual surrender was forced by the dropping of **atomic bombs** on Hiroshima and Nagasaki in August 1945 and Russia's declaration of war, followed by occupation of the Kuril Islands

The scene after an atomic bomb at Hiroshima. Two atomic bombs were dropped, one here and the other at Nagasaki. They were so powerful that they created huge fireballs that destroyed everything except concrete buildings.

(see page 4). Faced with the possibility of being divided between occupying powers and having the imperial court abolished, Japan finally laid down its arms and waited for the unknown.

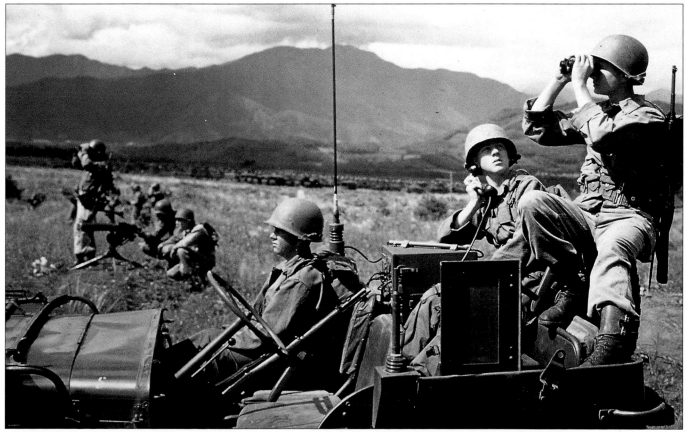

After Japan's surrender in 1945, the Allied forces moved into Japan and took control of the government.

6 The New Japan

Modernization

During the Allied **Occupation** of 1945–52, Japan adopted a new, democratic constitution that granted equal rights to all citizens, including women. Reforms were passed that improved education and gave land to farmers. As soon as the Occupation ended, Japan signed an alliance with her former enemy, the United States, which then became her biggest trading partner.

This *officially sponsored photograph represented an ideal view of the new, postwar Japan – the perfect timing of the super-express bullet train and the timeless perfection of Mount Fuji. This picture was published around the world in books and posters.*

Recovery

By 1955 the output of Japanese industry had risen to the levels of 1936. Rapid economic growth soon made Japan a world leader in shipbuilding, steel, cameras, and electrical goods. In 1958 Japan launched the world's largest oil tanker. By 1964 Japan was ready to go on show to the world as the host of a highly successful Olympic games. The bullet train service — at 120 miles (200 kilometers) per hour — that began that year became a symbol of Japan's efficiency and advanced technology. The first industrial robot came into use in 1970. Less welcome was the pollution that was a damaging side effect of industrial expansion.

Oil Shocks

The quadrupling of oil prices in 1973 hit Japan hard, because almost all of its energy was imported. In 1979 there was a second oil shock. Industry responded by cutting back on manufacturing that needed large amounts of oil – such as steel and chemicals – and expanding those that depended on skilled labor – such as electronics and computers. These high-tech industries had the advantage of causing far less pollution than oil-based industries.

The opening ceremony of the 1964 Olympic Games, hosted in Tokyo. The 19-year-old torch-bearer was born in Hiroshima on the day the atomic bomb was dropped.

Internationalization

By the 1970s Japanese companies were beginning to set up in business abroad, partly to be nearer their markets, partly to take advantage of lower prices for land, labor and materials. Northern Europe, the United States, and Southeast Asia were especially favored areas for Japanese **investment**. Japan also became the world's largest giver of foreign aid by 1988.

In 1992 a change in the law allowed 2,000 Japanese troops to operate overseas and take part in United Nations peacekeeping operations in Cambodia, mostly providing technical services as engineers. This was a small but important step for Japan in playing a much bigger part in tackling international problems.

Japan Today

Mass production of electrical goods made Japan's economy strong in the 1960s. Other important products were steel, ships, and cameras. Today Japan is a leading producer of computers and industrial robots.

Japan has progressed from the industries that built up its economy in the 1950s and 1960s, such as steel and shipbuilding, and is now a world leader in computers and electronics. More Japanese work in the service industries – retailing, transport, education, and medical care – than work in factories. And, while Japan does have some of the most advanced factories in the world, there are still hundreds of thousands of small workshops that either produce components for the big businesses or make traditional craft goods such as straw floor matting (tatami) or wooden clogs (geta).

Leisure

Japanese leisure is a mixture of the old and the new. Sumo wrestling has a great following, but so too does baseball, which was introduced to Japan by American missionaries over a century ago. Japanese are very proud that judo and kendo (Japanese fencing with bamboo swords) are now known around the world – but only 2 percent of Japanese actually take part in these sports. Tennis and volleyball are the main sports for women, but they also like to take part in traditional pastimes such as flower arranging and tea ceremonies. Most Japanese, especially women, can play a musical instrument of some sort, and a quarter of all homes possess a piano.

Kendo – the way of the sword. Japanese fencing, like other activities – judo, ikebana (flower arranging), origami (paper folding), and karaoke (sing-along)– have won enthusiastic fans around the world, as have the growing of miniature trees (bonsai) and the writing of haiku poems.

Politics

From 1955 until 1993 Japan was ruled by a single party, the Liberal Democrats. They were supported by big business, and their politicians were often accused of corruption for taking money from firms in return for favors. In 1993 a coalition of opposition parties came into power to reform the system but found this easier to promise than to put into practice. Meanwhile, a great deal of real power still rested with government officials.

Business and Pleasure

During the postwar period, Japanese brand names have become known around the world. More people can name half a dozen kinds of Japanese cars or cameras than could name a single Japanese politician, artist, or writer. Even more important, perhaps, is the fact that Japanese companies have set up businesses overseas – especially in the United States, Britain, and Southeast Asia. Where business goes, customs and fashions follow. Many cities have Japanese restaurants. Japanese designers exhibit in Paris. There are Western enthusiasts for origami (paper folding), carp breeding, and bonsai (miniature trees).

New discoveries will be made in the future as more and more people from around the world explore Japan.

The ultramodern high-tech architecture of industrialized Japan.

A display of kumade *on sale at a Shinto temple. They are good-luck charms.*

Time Chart

Japan	Europe	Other
c. 8000 B.C. First pottery made in Japan.	**c. 6500 B.C.** Farming begins in Greece and spreads to other areas of Europe.	**c. 9000 B.C.** Hunters spread throughout North and South America.
660 B.C. Traditional date of first emperor, Jimmu.	**c. 1600 B.C.** Mycenaean civilization begins in Greece.	**c. 650 B.C.** Iron is being used in China.
c. 400 A.D. Emergence of Yamato rule.	**452 A.D.** Attila the Hun enters Italy.	**30 A.D.** Death of Jesus Christ. The spread of Christianity begins.
c. 550 Introduction of Buddhism.	**542 A.D.** Bubonic plague spreads through Europe.	**622** Muhammad founds the religion of Islam in Arabia.
607 First official mission to China.	**597** St. Augustine lands in England with 30 missionaries.	**935** The text of the Koran finished.
741 Provinces ordered to build Buddhist monasteries.	**757** Offa becomes king of Mercia in England.	**c. 1000** The Vikings colonize Greenland and travel to North America.
1192 Shogun rule established.	**1066** The Normans conquer England.	**1352** Ibn Battuta travels to Africa.
1467 Beginning of civil wars.	**1492** The first globe is made in Germany by Martin Beheim.	**1368** Ming dynasty in China begins.
1543 First Europeans reach Japan.	**1532** John Calvin starts the Protestant movement in France.	**1492** Christopher Columbus reaches the Americas.
1590 Unification of Japan complete.	**1618** The Thirty Years War of religion starts.	**1607** The first English settlement is founded in America (Virginia).
1639 Japan closed to foreign contacts.	**1667** The French begin to expand under Louis XIV.	**1644** Manchu dynasty in China begins.
1853 Commodore Perry's ships open up Japan.	**1707** England and Scotland unite.	**1680** Rozvi Empire in Zimbabwe.
1868 The Meiji restoration	**1789** The French Revolution begins.	**1775** The American Revolution begins.
1889 New constitution adopted.	**1833** The slave trade is abolished in Britain.	**1789** George Washington becomes the first president of the United States.
1894-95 War against China.	**1884-85** The African conference is held in Berlin (Germany).	**c. 1700s** The European exploration of Africa begins.
1904-05 War against Russia.	**1901** Queen Victoria dies.	**1861** The American Civil War begins.
1910 Korea becomes a colony.	**1914-18** The First World War.	**1917** The United States enters World War I.
1941 Attack on Pearl Harbor.	**1939-45** The Second World War.	**1941** The United States enters World War II.
1972 Okinawa reverts to Japan.	**1961** The Berlin Wall is built in Germany.	**1961** John F. Kennedy becomes president of the USA.
1973 and **1979** Oil shocks.	**1972** The European Community gains more members.	**1963** John F. Kennedy is assassinated.
1986 Twelfth Summit Conference held in Tokyo.	**1985** Mikhail Gorbachev becomes the leader of the Soviet Union.	**1965-73** The United States is involved in the Vietnam War.
1989 Death of Emperor Hirohito (Showa).	**1989** Boris Yeltsin becomes leader of Russia.	**1981** Ronald Reagan becomes U.S. president.
1993 Marriage of Crown Prince Naruhito to a commoner, Miss Owada.	**1991** East and West Germany are united. The Berlin Wall is destroyed.	**1993** Bill Clinton become U.S. president.

Glossary

A

archaeologist: a person who studies the past by excavating ancient sites.

archipelago: a group of islands

armorer: a person who makes or mends arms, such as guns, and armor.

assassinate: to murder someone, usually a political figure.

atomic bomb: a type of bomb that is powered by a nuclear reaction.

B

beach: to run or haul a ship onto a beach or shore.

Buddhism: a religion begun by the Indian Gautama about 2,500 years ago. He said that by destroying greed and hatred, which are the causes of suffering, people may reach **enlightenment**.

C

calligraphy: the art of beautiful handwriting.

census: an official count of the population, including such information as people's age and occupation.

Confucius: a Chinese philosopher who lived about 551–479 B.C.E. He taught virtue and responsibility and the rightful place of everyone in society.

conscript: a person who is forced to sign up for military service.

constitution: the basic laws by which a state or nation is governed.

consul: an official who is appointed by his or her country to protect its business interests and look after its citizens in a foreign country.

convert: to cause someone to change his or her beliefs.

council: a group of people who have been elected or appointed to oversee administration and law.

cremate: to burn a dead body.

D

daimyo: important Japanese landowners who became warlords, making war against their neighbors.

diplomat: an official who negotiates for his or her country in a foreign country.

disciples: followers of particular leaders or teachings.

drill: in military terms, the training of soldiers in procedures such as the use of weapons.

E

economics: the study of finances and businesses.

embassy: the residence or place of business for any foreign official in a specific country.

enlightened: to have seen the light or truth of the matter.

excavate: to dig up in a methodical and scientific manner.

exports: goods that are sold abroad.

F

fortifications: especially strong defenses around cities or castles.

G

glacier: a slowly moving mass of ice.

governor: a senior administrator of a society.

guilds: an association of people, such as merchants, with the same interests.

I

imports: goods that are brought into a country from abroad.

investment: the act of putting money into projects.

J

Jesuit: a member of a Roman Catholic order. The order of the Jesuits was set up by Ignatius Loyola in 1534 to defend Catholicism against reform.

junk: a Chinese boat.

K

kimono: a loose-sashed, ankle-length garment with wide sleeves.

Kublai Khan: (c.1215–94), ruler of China and Mongolia, and grandson of Genghis Khan.

L

lacquer: a hard, glossy coating on decorative objects.

M

migrate: to go from one place to settle in another.

missionaries: people who try to **convert** others to their religion.

Mongols: people who come from Mongolia in central Asia.

O

Occupation: the period of Japanese history after the Second World War, when American forces lived in Japan.

P

persecute: to treat others badly because of their race or religion.

pronunciation: the way to say particular sounds.

province: an area ruled as a part of a country or state.

puppet state: a country that seems independent but is in fact controlled by another.

R

reforms: improvements made to existing rules and customs.

S

samurai: the Japanese warrior class that started in the 11th century. Samurai were prepared to fight and die for their **daimyos**, to whom they swore undying loyalty.

Shinto: the ancient Japanese religion meaning "the way of the gods." Its followers believed that spirits called *kami*, lived in gods, nature, and people.

shogun: a title given to a warlord meaning "great barbarian-conquering supreme general." Shoguns always came from the warrior class of the samurai.

survey: to plot a detailed view of an area of land.

T

taxes: an amount of money that everyone has to pay to the government.

treaty: a formal agreement between two or more states.

V

vaccination: a method of enabling people to resist dangerous diseases.

Index

Numbers in **bold** indicate an illustration. Words in **bold** are in the glossary on page 47.